The Treasure Map to Humble
Communication, Negotiation,
Arbitration, Mediation, and

Handling Confrontation
for Adults

Dr. Chad Costantino

Copyright © 2017

Abundant Life Publishing

All Rights Reserved. No part of this book may be reproduced in any form without permission in writing from the publisher, except in the case of brief quotations embodied in critical articles or reviews.

Edited by: Gavriela Powers

Assistant Editor: John Hall

Cover and Interior Design: Gavriela Powers

We hope you enjoy this book from Abundant Life Publishing. Our goal is to help you and your little ones live, laugh, and be the light of Yeshua (Jesus)!

Abundant Life Publishing

Salisbury, NC

Printed in the United States of America

Contents

Introduction 6
Chapter One 8
Chapter Two 15
Chapter Three 20
Chapter Four 25
Chapter Five 32
Chapter Six 37
Chapter Seven 41
Chapter Eight 47
Chapter Nine 54
Chapter Ten 62
Chapter Eleven 69
Chapter Twelve 76
Chapter Thirteen 83
Chapter Fourteen 88
Chapter Fifteen 94
Chapter Sixteen 99
Chapter Seventeen 105
Chapter Eighteen 110
Chapter Nineteen 117
Chapter Twenty 122
Chapter Twenty-One 126
The ABCs to Communication During Confrontation: 128
Twelve Steps for Dealing with Conflict 134

By Tamara Lowe 134

Abundant Life Publishing and Dr. Chad Costantino would like to give a special thanks to Tamara Lowe and the Kingdom Builder's Academy Inner Circle.

Introduction

Humble communication is essential to having success in relationships, business deals, and everyday life, including our spiritual life. Learning how to communicate with excellence and humility can be a lifelong endeavor, and should be something that every adult sets their mind to teaching themselves and their children.

Humble communication helps us build stronger connections with others; it also helps as achieve goals, build businesses, raise families, create peace, and many more things! Humility is something that is required in our communication with God (1 Peter 5:5-6), and without it, we may find ourselves at the end of our journey, lacking understanding and leaving an incomplete legacy.

Throughout this booklet we will offer diversified definitions to help the reader achieve the level of understanding in communication that is necessary, as well as include a short review at the end of each chapter for life application of humble communication.

Chapter One

Diversified Definition:

Conciliation. Conciliation is the process of settling arguments and disputes between believers outside of court in a Biblical manner.

Conciliation is used when Christian business owners have legal disputes and they desire to resolve the matter outside of court rather than subject one another to the non-Christian courtroom. Conciliation can be used for believers who are not business owners, but most legal disputes between believers arise from business matters that can cause pressure or trials in the faith of a Christian.

Christian business owners desire to operate their business according to the standards of the Bible and not the world; therefore, conciliation is extremely effective and popular among Christian business owners as a means of maintaining righteous standards of conduct in a business setting according to their faith.

Righteous and proper communication is extremely important in relationships of all kinds, and not just business relationships. Tone of voice and body language are part of proper communication as well; your body language and tone of voice should match what information you are communicating.

Conciliation involves up to three steps:

1. Each party is privately counseled on how to peacefully resolve situations using Biblical principles.
2. If private counseling is unsuccessful, each party would submit the situation to a mediator, which is someone who would go between each party to relay information and points of view using Biblical principles, teaching each party how to communicate constructively and resolve the situation.
3. If both first steps fail, then each party would submit the situation to an arbitrator, which is legally capable of settling a dispute.

Situations where conciliation would be necessary include but are not limited to:

Contract disputes, employment, family, church, personal injury, professional, landlord/tenant disputes, real estate disputes, creditor disputes, etc. Monetary value is not limited and can range from nothing to millions. Conciliation has proven to be successful and effective for many reasons, and has saved many people from the negative emotional consequences that can often arise due to a dispute between two parties for any reason.

> Humility is not thinking less of yourself, but thinking of yourself less.
>
> C.S. LEWIS

Conciliation services can range from $50 an hour to $350 an hour depending on the severity and expertise needed for the situation. Most conciliation services have payment options available for each financial situation the parties may encounter.

The important thing to remember about conciliation is the process in which it must take place to be effective. The Bible gives us a specific outline for how disputes should be handled between believers, and if not adhered to, the principle result is ineffective communication:

Matthew 18:15-17 (NLT), *"'If another believer sins against you, go privately and point out the offense. If the other person listens and confesses it, you have won that person back. But if you are unsuccessful, take one or two others with you and go back again, so that everything you say may be confirmed by two or three witnesses. If the person still refuses to listen, take your case to the church. Then if he or she won't accept the church's decision, treat that person as a pagan or a corrupt tax collector."*

- ☐ Disputes are always encouraged to be dealt with **privately** first, if possible.
- ☐ If not possible, two or three witnesses need to be called into the matter for validation.
- ☐ If that is unsuccessful, the matter is to be brought to the elders and council of the church.
- ☐ If the person still refuses to submit to the council and decision of the church after the entire process, they are to be treated as a pagan or a corrupt tax collector; this means lawful action is needed to settle the dispute, and Christian Conciliation has not been successful due to irreconcilable differences between the parties.

Cases where conciliation have proven successful in the past include (but are not limited to):

➢ A husband and wife were struggling with an impending divorce and seeking other routes before finalizing said divorce.
➢ Owners of a business could not come to an agreement about how to properly divide its assets.
➢ A company claimed that an infringement has been made on their copyright patent by another company.
➢ An employee claimed that he/she was improperly fired from their job.
➢ The owner of a house claimed the contracted builders defrauded them with defective work.
➢ A neighbor was frequently bothered by their neighbor's dog that barked late at night.
➢ The birth mother of a child wanted to reverse the adoption.
➢ A divorced couple disagrees continually on parenting plans for the children, visitation rights, and child support, etc.

When submitting to the process of conciliation, you will be expected to adhere to the following moral principles:

- ☐ Honesty: Ephesians 4:25
- ☐ Do what is just and merciful: Micah 6:8
- ☐ Accept responsibility for your actions and admit your wrongdoings: Matthew 7:5
- ☐ Keep your word: Matthew 5:37
- ☐ Put others interests before your own: Philippians 2:4
- ☐ Be a good listener: Proverbs 18:13
- ☐ Overlook minor offenses: Proverbs 19:11
- ☐ Confront others with humility and not pride: Ephesians 4:29
- ☐ Always be open to forgiveness and reconciliation: Ephesians 4:32
- ☐ Change harmful attitudes and behaviors: Proverbs 28:13
- ☐ Be willing to repay for any damage you may have caused: Exodus 21:33-34

Conciliation expects each party to submit to the following:

Matthew 7:12 (NLT), *"Do to others whatever you would like them to do to you. This is the essence of all that is taught in the law and the prophets."*

Review:

Can you think of a situation in your life right now that would benefit from conciliation? If so, what is the situation?

_____
_____
_____
_____

What else is important in communication other than the words we use?

_____
_____

What is the first step that conciliation promotes when it comes to a dispute between believers?

_____
_____
_____

Chapter Two
Diversified Definition:

Pledge. A pledge is a solemn promise or undertaking.

As a believer in Yeshua (Jesus), we have agreed to abide by His standards and His laws as our way of life. For unbelievers, the Bible offers an effective outline for how to handle disputes and communicate properly because the principles of the Bible are not limited to believers only. God's law is God's law no matter the belief of the individual.

As believers, however, we are to allow

> There is a thin line between confidence and arrogance. It's called humility. Confidence smiles; arrogance smirks.
>
> Author Unknown

ourselves to be held accountable to the standards of the Bible in all our ways of living. Communication is one of the most important subjects when it comes to relationships, because wrong communication can lead to the destruction of a God-ordained relationship.

We are called to be peacemakers by nature. Problem solvers. The ones with wisdom and peace from the Holy Spirit, allowing God's Spirit to lead and direct our actions instead of our emotions. The Bible gives us many standards to hold ourselves to when it comes to communication and relationships, and they all deal with keeping yourself humble and walking in love towards your God, self, and neighbor.

As believers in Yeshua (Jesus Christ) as the Son of God, we have pledged our lives to Him to obedience to His Word. His Word teaches us that conflicts are to be dealt with in a remarkably different way than the world (Luke 6:27-36, Matthew 5:9), and that conflicts provide an opportunity to glorify God, grow our spirits into maturity in Yeshua (Jesus), and serve others (1 Corinthians 10:31-11:1).

Pledge	Scripture
Glorify God First	Psalm 37:1-6, Mark 11:25, John 14:15, Romans 12:17-21, 1 Corinthians 10:31

Remain Humble	Proverbs 28:13, Matthew 7:3-5, Colossians 3:5-14
Restore with Gentleness	Proverbs 19:11, Matthew 18:15-20, Galatians 6:1-2
Reconciliation	Matthew 5:23-24, Matthew 6:12, Ephesians 4:1-3, Philippians 2:3-4

The Purposed Peace Pledge:

"By the grace of God and because I believe in and adhere to the principles taught by Yeshua (Jesus Christ), I **pledge** to be a peacemaker in communication in every relationship that I have been blessed with. I **pledge** to glorify God first by focusing on His desires instead of my own. I **pledge** to examine my own heart-motivations and shortcomings before pointing out a fault or annoyance to someone else. I **pledge** to confess my own sin first and ask the Holy Spirit to provide strength to change before expecting someone else to change first. I **pledge** to never speak ill of anyone behind their back and to overlook minor offenses for the sake of love and peace. I **pledge** to seek restoration over revenge, and to submit myself to conciliation when necessary. I **pledge** to seek the path of reconciliation at all costs, never compromising the moral principles of the Bible, and remaining humble in my communication and expectations of myself and others. I am a peacemaker. I am an excellent communicator who is solution-oriented and filled with the Holy Spirit."

Pledges should only be spoken in integrity of heart and not with ulterior motives. One's pledge is as good as their word, which should be valued higher than anything, as the Bible tells us to let our "yes be yes" and our "no be no". When a believer gives their pledge, it is thought to be as good as God's Word because we believe in Yeshua (Jesus) and are filled with the Holy Spirit and are held accountable to the standard of the Bible; in other words, **believers believe believers *because* we are believers**!

Review:

Instead of making decisions based off emotions, how should we make decisions?

_____

_____

_____

What do conflicts provide the opportunity to do?

_____

_____

_____

Why should a believer's pledge be as good as God's Word?
_____
_____
_____

Chapter Three

Diversified Definition:

Affidavit. An affidavit is a written statement confirmed by oath or affirmation, for use as evidence in court.

Affidavits are used in legal situations where the court needs a signed document stating the facts and evidence of the case. Affidavits are submitted as evidence because they are believed to be true and are signed by two or more witnesses that can verify the information was voluntarily written down and is sworn by the person writing the affidavit that it is truth.

In the process of humble communication, affidavits would only be needed in extreme legal cases where disputes were not able to be settled by Christian Conciliation. Even in the process of Christian Conciliation, it may be helpful to write out your statement of the true facts so that you have a point of reference for communication and reconciliation.

It is extremely important to remember that humble and successful communication for settling disputes is based in integrity. Both parties are expected to tell the truth and hold fast to the truth for the process to be effective. This means being willing to examine your own attitudes and heart motivations to make sure that you are not adding to or taking away from the truth.

Integrity is more important in communication than perhaps any other factor involved. If truth sets people free (John 8:32), then deception and lies keep people in bondage. Communicating with anything other than purity in motives of heart and integrity will cause strife, and perhaps even lead to bigger disasters in the long run.

Lies have a way of tangling people into a giant mess. Lies are hard to keep track of and even harder to continue to cover as time goes on. The truth has a natural way of revealing itself in time (Luke 12:3), therefore humble communication is always rooted and grounded in integrity and truth.

> Pride is about MY glory; humility is about GOD'S glory.
>
> Author Unknown

Lies create confrontations while truth solves them. When dealing with issues of integrity, it is best to hold fast to the truth always and gently (or firmly if needed, but not rudely) stand your ground when confronting a situation where someone has lied about something and it has caused an issue.

Confrontations don't have to be messy, rude, or even heated. The attitude of integrity that you bring into the confrontation will determine the overall atmosphere of the conversation; your disposition of lovingly walking in integrity and truth can truly put someone else at ease and help them to confront and face their own faults and methods of communicating.

You are in control of everything you say and everything you do. No one else determines what you say and do; that is ultimately left up to you! You don't have to allow anyone else's disposition of lies or lack of integrity determine your level of integrity in communication. You can decide to continue walking in the truth humbly and keeping your tone of voice even and your attitude calm even if the other person is raging and ranting!

I won't say that it's easy, but it is simple. Walking and keeping yourself accountable morally will increase the quality of your life and create an even better quality of life for those in your sphere of influence.

Guidelines for writing an Affidavit:

1. The affidavit must be signed in front of two witnesses. These two witnesses must be people that can verify the facts and statements in the affidavit are true. 2 Corinthians 13:1, *"In the mouth of two or three witnesses, every word shall be established."*
2. The person writing the affidavit (you) must make a statement of acknowledgement that everything you have written is true, complete, and whole. Matthew 5:37, *"Let your yes be yes and your no be no."*
3. The person writing the affidavit must state the location and date of where the document is being signed.

Review:

What is one of the most important aspects of humble communication?

_____
_____
_____

What do lies create?

_____

_____

_____

What are three ways you can improve your integrity?

_____

_____

_____

Chapter Four

Diversified Definition:

Law. A law is a rule of action, or any regulation that applies to a situation or action or establishment.

Law was created to bring order to chaotic situations. Law was created to give mankind a threshold of understanding the difference between what is considered acceptable and unacceptable.

God's word is a lamp unto our feet and a light unto our paths (Psalm 119:105); within His word He has given us several statutes and laws to live by, which help illuminate our paths as we stay on the straight and narrow road towards redemption (Matthew 7:14).

In the natural world, we also have governing laws we must abide by according to whatever country or state we live in. Generally, law is divided into four main classes:

- The Law of Nature

- International Law
- Public Law
- Private Law

Within each of these main classes of law, we find even more divisions of law that help us break it down into very specific details about situations, regulations, rules, and guidelines. The three primary jurisdictions of law, which are according to their location: Common Law (these laws vary by states), Equity (this is used when Common Law is too harsh and not justified), and Admiralty and Maritime (these apply to situations that happened in navigable waters).

> Pride is concerned with who is right. Humility is concerned with what is right.
>
> Ezra Taft Benson

The Constitution is the fundamental law of the state, which gives us the principles that birthed the foundation of the United States government, regulations for each division of its sovereign power, directions for whom these powers are given to and how they are to be exercised.

In the same manner, the Word of God is like our constitution of faith. It gives us the fundamental laws of the heavens and how the power is distributed and used according to those in the faith. The Word of God gives us laws regarding humble communication, and when followed, these laws produce an abundance of life without strife and filled with peace.

The Word of God also shows us what happens when we do not abide by the laws of humble communication: death, destruction, confusion, chaos, pain, sorrow, grief, broken relationships, even spiritual poverty!

God's Laws of Humble Communication:

- ✓ Psalm 19:14 communication law says, "Let the <u>words of my mouth and the meditation of my heart Be acceptable in Your sight</u>, O LORD, my rock and my Redeemer."
- ✓ Psalm 39:1 communication law says, "I said, "I will guard my ways <u>That I may not sin with my tongue</u>; I will guard my mouth as with a muzzle While the wicked are in my presence."

- ✓ Ephesians 4:29-31 communication law says, "<u>Let no unwholesome word proceed from your mouth</u>, but only such a word as is good for edification according to the need of the moment, so that it will give grace to those who hear. Do not grieve the Holy Spirit of God, by whom you were sealed for the day of redemption. Let all bitterness and wrath and anger and clamor and slander be put away from you, along with all malice."
- ✓ Proverbs 4:24 communication law says, "<u>Put away from you a deceitful mouth and put devious speech far from you</u>."
- ✓ Ephesians 5:4 communication law says, "and there must be no filthiness and silly talk, or coarse jesting, which are not fitting, <u>but rather giving of thanks</u>."
- ✓ Colossians 3:8-10 communication law says, "But now you also, put them all aside: anger, wrath, malice, slander, and abusive speech from your mouth. <u>Do not lie to one another</u>, since you laid aside the old self with its evil practices, and have put on the new self who is being renewed to a true knowledge according to the image of the One who created him—"

- ✓ 1 Peter 3:9-10 communication law says, "<u>not returning evil for evil or insult for insult, but giving a blessing instead</u>; for you were called for the very purpose that you might inherit a blessing. For, "THE ONE WHO DESIRES LIFE, TO LOVE AND SEE GOOD DAYS, MUST KEEP HIS TONGUE FROM EVIL AND HIS LIPS FROM SPEAKING DECEIT.""
- ✓ Colossians 3:17 communication law says, "Whatever you do in word or deed, do all in the name of the Lord Jesus, <u>giving thanks</u> through Him to God the Father."
- ✓ Psalm 34:12-13 communication law says, "Who is the man who desires life and loves length of days that he may see good? <u>Keep your tongue from evil and your lips from speaking deceit</u>."

God's Communication Law Do's and Don'ts:

Do	Don't
Make your words (and attitude) line up with God's Word.	Speak negative projections of others or self.

Guard your mouth when in the presence of wickedness.	Sin with your tongue and say just anything that pops into your head.
Speak only edifying (good, encouraging) words that give grace.	Let any unwholesome word come out of your mouth, or grieve the Holy Spirit.
Speak truth always.	Speak deceitfully.
Continually give thanks to God through Yeshua (Jesus Christ).	Speak filthy or silly words.
Put aside abusive speech and anger.	Lie to one another.

Review:

What are three communication laws you already achieve?

_____

_____

_____

What are three communication laws you could do better in?

_____

_____

_____

How is the Word of God like a Constitution for our faith?

_____

_____

_____

Chapter Five
Diversified Definition:

Principle. When you think of a "principle", think about the question, "Where am I coming from?". A principle is a fundamental truth or doctrine that is settled, clear, and unchangeable morally.

Principles are important in humble communication because they ask the question, "Where am I coming from?", or "Where is the other person coming from?" These questions are important to understand the answers to when facing a confrontation of any kind.

> Speak in such a way that others love to listen to you. Listen in such a way that others love to speak to you.
>
> Author Unknown

Understanding the principles of humble communication will allow you to make humble communication your first choice instead of last!

The principles of humble communication lie within the Word of God. We choose to humbly communicate because of our love and belief in Him. The principle of our communication should always be as simple as this: is what I am communicating wrong, or right? Here are some Scriptures to help you understand why the foundation of your communication is important:

- All the ways of a man are clean in his own eyes, but the Lord weighs the motives (Proverbs 16:2)
- The Lord searches the heart, tests the mind, even to give to each man according to his ways, according to the result of his deeds (Jeremiah 17:10)
- God alone knows the hearts of all the sons of men (1 Kings 8:39)
- The Lord searches all hearts and understands every intent of the thoughts, and if you seek Him He will let you find Him, but if you forsake Him, He will reject you forever (1 Chronicles 28:9)
- The Lord does not look as a man looks to the outward appearance to see; He looks at the heart (1 Samuel 16:7)

As the Bible clearly shows us, our heart motivations of communication are more important to God than the subject content of what we are communicating!

When facing confrontations or disagreements of any kind with anyone, it is important to examine the principle behind the argument: is the confrontation coming about because of moral issues, or is it a matter of opinions?

Here are some questions you can ask yourself in the heat of the moment while facing confrontation of any kind:

- ☐ Is the principle of the confrontation moral, or opinionated?
- ☐ If the confrontation is moral, how can both parties come together to agree on what is morally acceptable? Is the Bible the foundation of discussion?
- ☐ Am I keeping my tone of voice calm and even, or stressful and high-pitched or paced?
- ☐ Are my words carefully planned, thought about and purposed, or irrational and off-the-cuff?
- ☐ Is the principle of my communication in this confrontation backed up by a Biblical foundation, or my own opinion/preferences of things?

- ☐ Is the principle of this confrontation, aimed around elevating myself and my own opinion, or elevating God and His Word?
- ☐ Can my opinion, preference, or point of view be found in the Bible, and if so, what does the Bible say about it?
- ☐ Is the other person in the confrontation willing to submit to Biblical principles, and if not, how can we come to an agreement or solution otherwise?
- ☐ What kind of compromise does the solution to this confrontation demand on my morals?
- ☐ Am I making sure that my body language is promoting comfort and peace, or am I being overbearing and intimidating?
- ☐ Have I prayed about this confrontation and conflict?

Review:

What confrontations have I had recently where I was not standing on a Biblical principle?

_____
_____
_____

What is the basis of all my communication?

_____

_____

_____

Do I try to see the other person's perspective first when in a confrontation, or am I too focused on my own perspective?

_____

_____

_____

Chapter Six

Diversified Definition:

Precept. When you think of a "precept", think about the question, "Where am I now?". A precept is an imposing standard of conduct or action.

The precepts of humble communication demand that the confrontation or discussion is relevant to the present or future, and not rooted in issues of the past that are irrelevant. A lot of confrontations are results of things that haven't been properly dealt with from the past that now affect the present and future.

It is advisable that past grievances that have not been dealt with that are not a matter of life or death simply be forgiven and moved beyond rather than confronted and hashed out, especially if the result of the confrontation would not surmount to a positive outcome.

The precept of any communication should be, "Where am I now?" and "How does this affect the future?" not, "I'm too hurt to move past this and I demand a confrontation!".

Any communication that does not benefit the present or future should be avoided and forgotten about, otherwise it can cause strife and discord that disrupts the present and hinders the future.

A precept is a commandment for an authoritive rule of action; your precepts for communication and confrontation should always be founded in humility and present or future tense concerns rather than looking back on the past. The past is beneficial to us only if we can learn from it.

> Communication is the key and saying your words with kindness is the way to go.
>
> Pamela Cummins

Things that we cannot change about the past are either powerless or powerful; if we give them rule over our today, they become the power of tomorrow. If we do not allow them rule and instead focus on where we are now, the power of tomorrow is had today!

The Bible says the precepts of man are vain (Matthew 15:9, Mark 7:7), but the precepts of the Lord are right and give joy to the heart (Psalm 19:8). Here is how you can test your precepts of communication:

- ☐ Is the confrontation I am facing relevant to what I am going through right now, or a root issue from the past?
- ☐ Will the precept of my communication lead to a positive or negative result?
- ☐ How have my past communication precepts gotten me to where I am now?
- ☐ How has my communication led to or contributed to a dispute or argument, and how can my communication be applied to help towards a positive result?
- ☐ What is the precept of my present communication, and will it benefit myself or others?
- ☐ I am a different person today than I was in the past. How different are the precepts of my communication today compared to those of the past?

Review:

What are my current precepts for communication?

_____

_____

_____

What situation am I going through right now that has been caused by something in the past?

_____

_____

_____

How can I be more present and future minded instead of past minded?

_____

_____

_____

Chapter Seven

Diversified Definition:

Purpose. When you think of a "purpose", think about the question, "Where am I going?". A purpose is that which one sets out to accomplish or attain.

Humans are born with the innate desire to understand their purpose and reason for living. Some give up the investigative mindsets and simply accept life as it is, and others make it their life's goal to make a mark and positive change in this world while they are here.

Discovering your purpose isn't easy, but it can be simple. Humble communication helps give us a smaller perspective of purpose in our everyday lives so we can more readily grasp the bigger picture. When we achieve humble communication, we are fulfilling purpose for today and tomorrow!

Every confrontation, discussion, and communication has a purpose. In humble communication, those purposes are not hidden, but made obvious and plain for both parties so there are no looming questions in the background about intention and direction. Humble communication makes purpose clear and concise, which also makes attaining a solution simpler and a more peaceful experience.

Before opening a confrontation or discussion, it is important that you first understand your heart purpose and motivation for doing so, the why behind your words and actions. If you decide to simply act based on your emotions without a solid purpose, you can find yourself creating chaos and confusion for others as well.

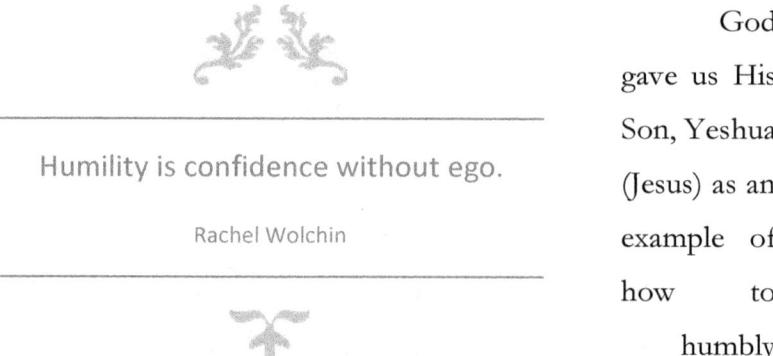

Humility is confidence without ego.

Rachel Wolchin

God gave us His Son, Yeshua (Jesus) as an example of how to humbly communicate with clear purpose and direction. Although Yeshua (Jesus) often spoke in parables, even that had a purpose and reason to it! Everything God does is for a purpose, and He is always certain of His purpose and goal before acting.

Proverbs 19:21 reminds us that a person has many plans in their heart, but it is the Lord's *purpose* that prevails. Before we begin a confrontation, we should examine the purpose behind every word we desire to speak. We should ask the Lord to show us His purpose in the matter, and if He is

not to be found in the situation, neither should we!

Humble communication is always purposed, precise, and simple. It's not the quantity of the words but the quality of which they are spoken, the purpose of which they are born, and the simplicity in which they are delivered that bring about the most fitting outcome for both listener and speaker.

1.) Know Your Why: Understand both God's and your own purpose behind the words you speak in your communication or confrontation. Place a higher priority on God's purpose so your heart intentions are founded in righteousness.

2.) Discipline Your Words: Choose the right words according to the leading of the Holy Spirit and not your flesh. Do not allow yourself to speak out of abundance of emotion, but purpose and precision.

3.) Face Fears: Realize your biggest fears in confrontation and face them head-on. Knowing your purpose in communication and confrontation will help you stay focused and push beyond fear!

4.) Find Faith: Your firm-footed action of purpose in communication should line up with your life beliefs and morals. Those that don't should be weeded out and replaced with proper faith!

5.) Have Gratitude: Speak words that resonate your humility and thankfulness. Refuse words that promote strife and stress and induce negative emotions. Gratitude edifies both speaker and listener!

6.) Know When to Say No: Saying yes to help others is a privilege, and we should extend ourselves regularly for others. Knowing when to say no, however, is also important, otherwise you can overextend yourself. Humbly communicating a "no" would include a gratitude sandwich: "Thank you for thinking of me to help you, and please understand I would love to be there for you. However, my priorities are full now and I would be unable to serve you in the best capacity that you need and deserve. Thank you again for thinking of me, and please consider asking me for help should you need it again in the future!" You show gratitude, give your reason for saying no, and end in gratitude.

Review:

What are my biggest fears in confrontation?

_____
_____
_____

Do my actions in how I currently handle confrontation reflect my morals and beliefs properly?

_____
_____
_____

Am I currently overextended from not knowing when to say no? How can I balance myself better in communication?

_____
_____
_____

Chapter Eight

Diversified Definition:

Confrontation. A confrontation is a hostile or argumentative meeting or situation between opposing parties.

How do confrontations arise between people? Isn't it from unmet desires and needs? The Bible says so in James 4:1-2:

"What is causing the quarrels and fights among you? Don't they come from the evil desires at war within you? You want what you don't have, so you scheme and kill to get it. You are jealous of what others have, but you can't get it, so you fight and wage war to take it away from them. Yet you don't have what you want because you don't ask God for it."

Even good desires can spring into something bad when our heart motivations and intentions change from pure to impure. Examples of an impure heart motivation towards achieving a desire or meeting a need would be trying to manipulate someone else's will to get what you want, being willing to sacrifice another's wellbeing to get what you want, etc.

In the life of adults, confrontations can be much worse than they ever were as kids on the playground fighting over territories and lunchbox treats. As adults, confrontations can often result in serious consequences if not handled properly – such as jail time, prison time, permanent destruction of relationships, etc.

That's why learning humble communication in how to handle confrontations is extremely vital to the adult life, even if there are no business aspects to it. Everyday relationships with our family members, friends, children, lovers, etc. demand a level of humble communication and proper confrontation handling to stay alive and flourish. Wrong tones of voices, attitudes, and body language in confrontations can harm relationships to the maximum degree.

> It was pride that changed angels into devils; it is humility that makes men as angels.
>
> Saint Augustine

Often when adults are facing confrontations, their emotions have them focusing on one thing alone: proving their point, proving they are right, and invalidating the other person's perspective to take top priority. A lot of adult confrontations end miserably because of selfishness and the lack of what I like to call, "Fighting Fair".

Fighting Fair in adult confrontations is about remaining humble, validating the other party's concerns and points of view, and communicating with excellence. Confrontations tend to escalate for the worst when either party is trying to invalidate the other party's point of view, emotions, etc. Each party has the desire of being heard and feeling important, which is what humble communication accomplishes.

Rules to Fighting Fair:

1.) Walk away, calm down, and pray.
2.) Speak calmly.
3.) Sit down together.
4.) Listen without interrupting.
5.) Detox! Get it out!
6.) Acknowledge your own faults.
7.) Focus on Biblical solutions, and get into agreement with God.
8.) Focus on weekly goals.
9.) Acknowledge your love for one another.
10.) Pray together!

If emotions are too high-strung and getting in the way of clear thinking, it is important to walk away, calm down, and pray. Both parties need to maintain an even attitude, tone of voice, and body language to humbly communicate.

Fighting Fair is about speaking calmly. Your emotions may be gripping you on the inside, but you must remain in control of your tone and pace of voice. If you are having a hard time not yelling or having an urgency in your tone or body language, change what you are thinking about! Instead of being uptight about being heard, make it a priority to calm down and hear the other person first.

Sit down together. Standing during confrontations can make the other party feel intimidated, or easily distracted. Find a quiet, calm place to sit down together, and maybe put a little soft praise and worship music in the background. Change the atmosphere from fearful to peaceful.

When the other person is speaking, listen without interrupting. Don't hear one word they say and allow your emotions to get in the way so you stop listening and are too focused on saying what you want to say. Empty your thoughts of yourself and intently listen to their perspective, and put yourself in their shoes. Listening puts out the message that you care and the other party is important.

Detox! Get it out! In a healthy manner, with a calm voice. Say what needs to be said in love, choose your words carefully, and do not put assumptions or projections onto the other person. Say how you feel and don't make it the other person's fault. Stay away from phrases like, "You *make* me feel…" or any other terms that places responsibility of your emotions and actions onto the other person. Make sure when you make statements you say they are your opinions and do not present them as infallible truth. Humble communication is about having the willingness to change your perspective if it is wrong, and helping both parties come to a favorable outcome.

Acknowledge your own faults. Do not talk about the other person's faults without first acknowledging your own. Own up to the things you are aware of that you do wrong, and ask the other person to help keep you lovingly accountable for other things you do wrong that you may not see clearly. Admit to your mistakes and faults and ask for forgiveness. Maintain an attitude of humility by realizing that you are as imperfect as the other person.

Focus on Biblical solutions and get into agreement with God. Seek and destroy the mindsets and words you are using that do not line up with God's Word. If your emotions are negative, take the time to fill yourself with positive reminders of God's promises and work on changing how you feel by changing what you're thinking about.

Focus on weekly goals. Don't overwhelm yourself with too many things to fix at once. Prioritize what the most important solutions are first, and go from there.

Acknowledge your love for one another. Always check your heart attitude against the Biblical definition of love and make sure your actions, words, tone of voice, and body language are promoting your belief in love. Uplift the other person. Speak gratitude for them.

End every confrontation with prayer! Never leave a confrontation without praying with and for one another. Seal the deal and the solution by inviting God into the equation and asking for His help in implementing the solution. Ask Him to bless the other person and your relationship. End on a positive note!

These ten steps are golden instructions for Fighting Fair and making sure you're lining up with what God desires for you in each confrontation situation. Fighting Fair is about pleasing God and implementing Biblical solutions!

Review:

What are three rules to Fighting Fair that I could be better at?

_____

_____

_____

What are three rules to Fighting Fair that I already practice daily?

_____

_____

_____

What confrontation in my past has happened as a result of not Fighting Fair?

_____

_____

_____

Chapter Nine

Diversified Definition:

Negotiation. A negotiation is a discussion aimed at reaching an agreement.

Negotiation is a cooperative bargaining process in which both parties come with a willing attitude to settle disputes and differences through a series of compromises and discussions. This is a conversation that is aimed at coming to an agreement that legitimately and favorably meets the needs of each party involved in the negotiation.

Philippians 2:4 states that we should not each look merely to our own interests, but to the interests of others as well. So, while it is important before entering negotiation with anyone to know your own stance and preferred outcome, it is just as important to have an open heart and mind to receive what the other person needs as well.

Before negotiations, prepare your attitude and emotions. Have the mindset of peacemaking. Train yourself to have the proper body language and understand that the entire point of negotiating is not merely getting your own way about things, but coming to a favorable solution for all parties involved.

Below is a Negotiation Focus Flow Chart:

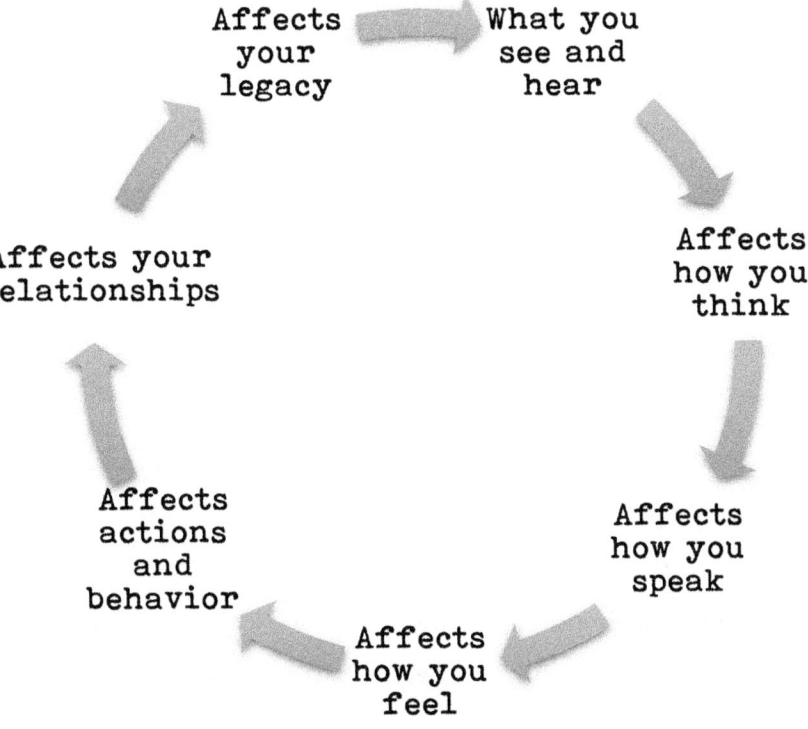

What you see and hear affects how you think. It's important to receive sound advice, opinions, and counsel from others who are experienced in negotiating if it is your first time needing to participate. It is equally as important to guard yourself against inexperienced advice, opinions from others that are based and spoken emotionally, and any ill-speaking of the other party you are negotiating with. If you come into a negotiation with the wrong mindset or attitude, it is likely to cause failure and stress.

What you think affects how you speak. If you're thinking ill of the other party or too highly of yourself, it will affect your speech. The tone of voice you use when speaking is as important as the words you choose to speak. If your thinking is rooted in negativity or faulty advice, it will show in your tone as well as your body language.

> Humility isn't denying your strengths; it's being honest about your weaknesses.
>
> Rick Warren

How you speak affects how you feel; your emotions begin with the thought process solidified once spoken, and ultimately finalized once acted upon through actions and behaviors. Your actions and behaviors affect your relationships, both personal and professional, which ultimately affects the outcome of your legacy.

In the negotiation process, it is important to remember to enter the situation with a fresh, positive mind that is seeking a peaceful solution; taking care of your mindset from the beginning will result in proper speech, emotions, actions and behaviors, and stronger relationships which will result in a rock-solid legacy!

Great negotiators are solid in their Kingdom Identity and know how to properly apply Kingdom Principles; this equals Kingdom Authority!

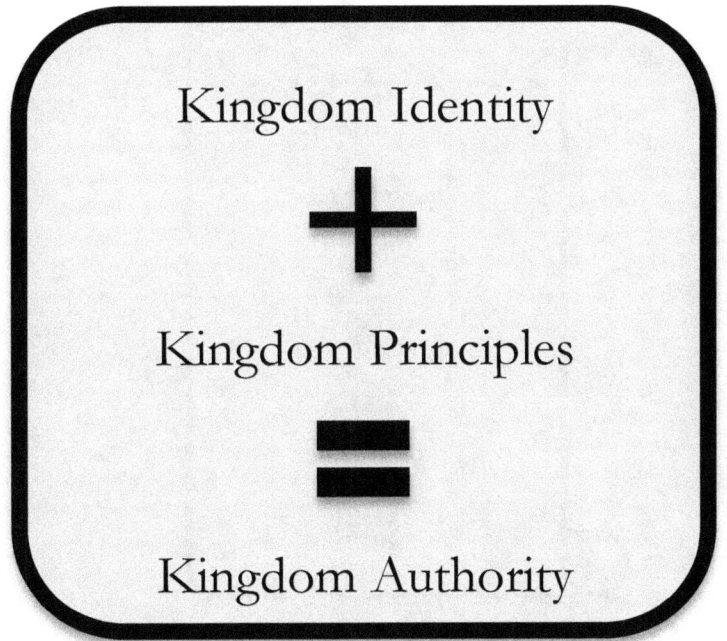

Kingdom Authority is the supernatural anointing of the Holy Spirit in all that you do, giving you authority over darkness. Negotiations between believers can sometimes get infiltrated with the enemy's attitudes and demonic influences, so being a successful negotiator between believers means being solid and assured of your Kingdom Identity, Kingdom Principles, and how to apply them. When it comes to negotiating, it's more than just a conversation; it's spiritual warfare!

Formula for God's Favor in Negotiations:

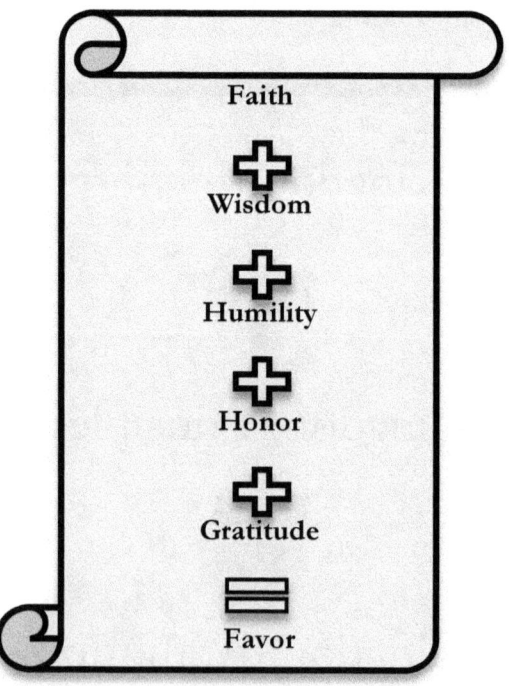

Faith: Hebrews 11:1&6 (NLT) says, *"Faith shows the reality of what we hope for; it is the evidence of things we cannot see. And it is impossible to please God without faith. Anyone who wants to come to him must believe that God exists and that he rewards those who sincerely seek him."* When you enter a negotiation with faith in the Holy Spirit to help you through, you're on the right track!

Wisdom: Proverbs 4:7 (NLT) says, *"Getting wisdom is the wisest thing you can do! And whatever else you do, develop good judgment."* Utilizing the wisdom you have gained from the Bible is essential to successful negotiation.

Humility: James 4:6-10 (NLT) says, *"And he gives grace generously. As the Scriptures say, 'God opposes the proud but gives grace to the humble.' So humble yourselves before God. Resist the devil, and he will flee from you. Come close to God, and God will come close to you. Wash your hands, you sinners; purify your hearts, for your loyalty is divided between God and the world. Let there be tears for what you have done. Let there be sorrow and deep grief. Let there be sadness instead of laughter, and gloom instead of joy. Humble yourselves before the Lord, and he will lift you up in honor."* Humility is essential to the negotiation process because God resists the proud!

Honor: Romans 13:1-2 (NLT) says, *"Everyone must submit to governing authorities. For all authority comes from God, and those in positions of authority have been placed there by God. So anyone who rebels against authority is rebelling against what God has instituted, and they will be punished."* Honor is important in the negotiation process because each party is coming together to *honor* one another's needs. Negotiation is not fashioned to help people demand their own way, but to help people come together to find the best way possible for all parties.

Gratitude: 1 Thessalonians 5:18 (NLT) says, *"Be thankful in all circumstances, for this is God's will for you who belong to Christ Jesus."* Gratitude is important in the negotiation process because gratitude brings about a peaceful atmosphere and an easy spirit. When each party is already grateful for what they have, it's easier to come together to negotiate needs and be good stewards of those things they're grateful for.

Favor: Proverbs 12:2 says, *"A good man will obtain favor from the LORD, But He will condemn a man who devises evil."* All these things placed together in the negotiation process equal and open a doorway for God's favor to come into the situation for all parties to seal the deal. Being led by the Holy Spirit ensures God's favor, and is vital to acquiring it. God uses His Spirit and His Kingdom Principles to lead the way to His way of life in Yeshua (Jesus). If you are entering a negotiation situation, make sure to bring these things to the table in your heart and attitude, and you're sure to bring the favor of God into the situation as well!

Review:

What are some Scripture verses you can think of to remind you of your Kingdom Identity?

_____

_____

_____

What is the main objective of peaceful negotiation?

_____

_____

_____

What are some Scripture verses you can think of to remind you of some important Kingdom Principles?

_____

_____

_____

When you think of "Kingdom Authority", what comes to mind?

_____

_____

_____

Chapter Ten

Diversified Definition:

Fear. An unpleasant emotion caused by the belief that someone or something is dangerous, likely to cause pain, or a threat.

Fear is one of the main sources of a communication gone wrong. Fear puts images and beliefs in our thoughts of suspected punishment, pain, or danger. Although in conversations it's not always the people we are afraid of, but how they might perceive what we are saying, how we look; sometimes we fear their opinion of us, their judgment of us, or we fear being misunderstood.

Whatever the root of the fear may be, fear has no place in humble communication. To humbly communicate, we must learn how to deal with fear properly, how to recognize it at its onset, and how to have grace when others are being fearful and help walk them through the process of dealing with it, too. In some of my adult experience, I fear people not listening to me, believing me, or simply not caring about what I have to say.

Since I am a writer and humble communication is part of my daily job, I take words and the efforts put into choosing those words very seriously.

The Bible gives us great Kingdom Principles about how to overcome fear. Let's look at a few of them:

> Humility is the mother of giants. One sees great things from the valley; only small things from the peak.
>
> G.K. Chesterson

- ✓ **Studying the Bible continually and meditating on its words helps you overcome fear by placing your thoughts in heavenly places instead of earthly places.**

Joshua 1:8-9 (NLT): *"Study this Book of Instruction continually. Meditate on it day and night so you will be sure to obey everything written in it. Only then will you prosper and succeed in all you do. This is my command—be strong and courageous! Do not be afraid or discouraged. For the Lord your God is with you wherever you go.""*

- ✓ **Fanning the flames of your spiritual gifts will help you overcome fear by keeping you passionate and** emblazed with hope in the Holy Spirit. You will feel more productive and confident.

2 Timothy 1:6-7 (NLT): *"This is why I remind you to fan into flames the spiritual gift God gave you when I laid my hands on you. For God has not given us a spirit of fear and timidity, but of power, love, and self-discipline."*

- ✓ **Obeying the Commands of the Bible will help you overcome fear because you will be walking in obedience, favor, and grace. When you are lined up and in obedience, there is nothing to fear!**

Matthew 28:20 (NLT): *"Teach these new disciples to obey all the commands I have given you. And be sure of this: I am with you always, even to the end of the age.""*

- ✓ **Remembering you are covered in the Blood of the Lamb and sharing your testimony in Him will help you overcome fear and humbly communicate because you will be emboldened by speaking truth!**

Revelation 12:11 (NLT): *"And they have defeated him by the blood of the Lamb and by their testimony. And they did not love their lives so much that they were afraid to die."*

- ✓ **Praying will help you overcome fear because it opens a doorway for the Holy Spirit to come in and help you humbly communicate when you are having troubles doing so.**

John 14:16 (NLT), *"And I will ask the Father, and he will give you another Advocate, who will never leave you."*

- ✓ **Knowing your Kingdom Identity will help you overcome fear in humble communication because you will understand your value and worth in Him, therefore treat others with value and worth.**

Luke 10:19-21 (NLT), *"Look, I have given you authority over all the power of the enemy, and you can walk among snakes and scorpions and crush them. Nothing will injure you. But don't rejoice because evil spirits obey you; rejoice because your names are registered in heaven.""*

Sometimes, especially as babies learning how to communicate properly, we feel so afraid and nothing we do makes the feeling of fear go away. In instances like this, it is important that we understand how to move forward despite the feeling of fear, and "Faith It".

When fear hits and you can't shake the feeling, you can still humbly communicate by: *seeing* the peaceful conversation in your heart. *Thinking* on the peaceful conversation before it has happened. *Believing* it will be peaceful. *Speaking* it peacefully. *Releasing* your hold on it. *Write* out your humble communication. *Fight* for a peaceful conversation and don't give up easily because of emotions. *Light* it with God's Word. *Confirm* it by taking steps to humbly communicate despite feelings of fear. Finally, *faith* it! When feelings of fear remain, recognize them for what they are, and move on!

Humble communication is not merely about overcoming your own fears, but having discernment in how to help others overcome theirs as well. Sometimes merely living and communicating by example is enough to help change someone else's life or solve someone else's problem. Other times, more proactive efforts are needed.

Faith It Flow Chart

→ → → →

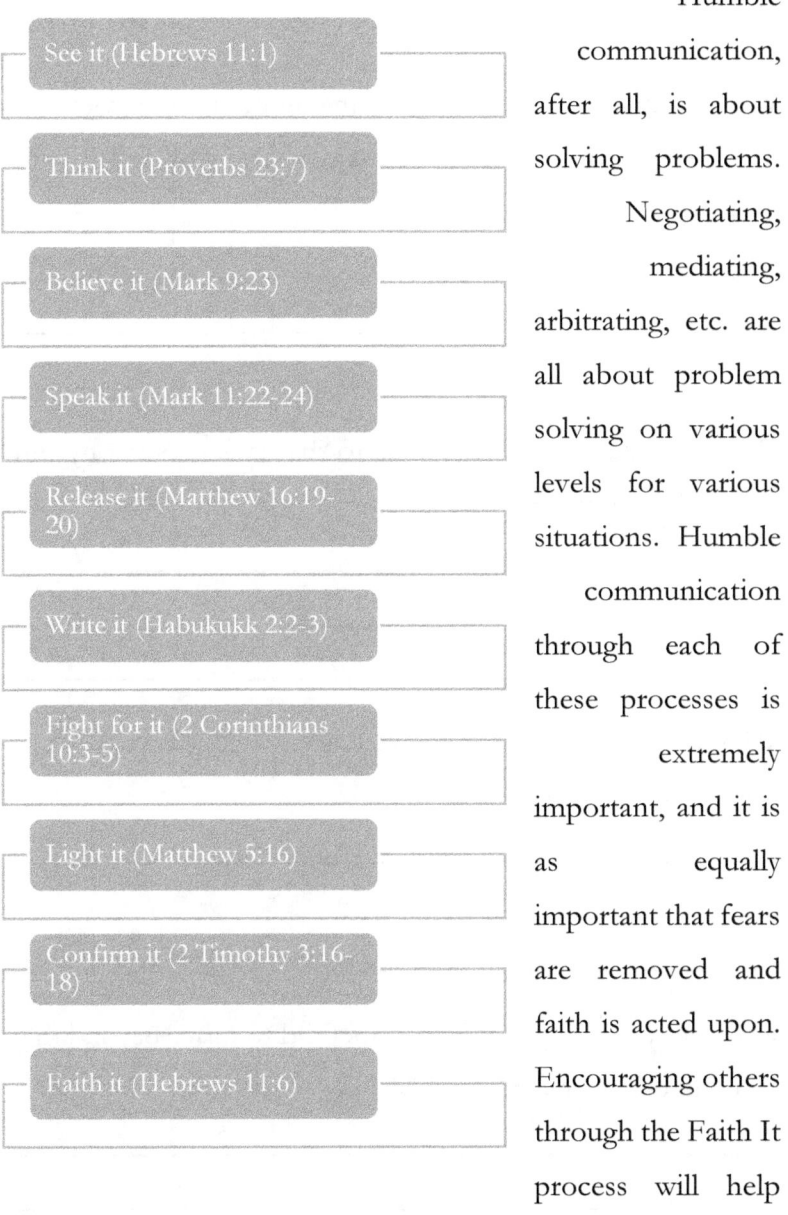

Humble communication, after all, is about solving problems. Negotiating, mediating, arbitrating, etc. are all about problem solving on various levels for various situations. Humble communication through each of these processes is extremely important, and it is as equally important that fears are removed and faith is acted upon. Encouraging others through the Faith It process will help them be able to move forward through their fears as well!

Review:

What is one of your biggest fears in communicating with other people, or maybe just a certain person who makes you nervous?

_____
_____
_____

Do you currently make it a habit to share your testimony with others? If not, why?

_____
_____
_____

What is a conversation you have been avoiding in your life right now due to fear?

_____
_____
_____

How can you apply the Faith It method to move beyond that fear and communicate humbly?

_____
_____
_____

Chapter Eleven

Diversified Definition:

Thought. Inward reasonings and the workings of conscious. Idea or conception. Opinion or judgment.

One of the very first things that I learned as a baby Christian was that our thoughts are influenced by either the Holy Spirit, or the enemy. Our thoughts are a product of what we

> Humbleness comes from an inner strength knowing who we are and our purpose; to not flaunt, but simple be who we were meant to be.
>
> Satsuki Shibuya

allow ourselves to meditate on repeatedly in the mind. Our thoughts can originate from a desire, a need, a judgment or an opinion.

Most people do not know this, but it is entirely possible to control your thoughts. You may not be able to help what comes into your mind sometimes, but you can always help what you allow to stay in your mind. The Bible refers to this as "taking every thought captive into the obedience of Messiah" (2 Corinthians 10:5).

Controlling your thoughts is a vital step to successfully communicating in humility no matter if you are acting as a mediator between two people, resolving your own personal problems, or negotiating with someone. Once you have allowed your thoughts to become angry, it is a lot harder to control angry emotions and words. Keeping your thoughts even, centered, and focused on Kingdom Principles is a great way to ensure that your communication comes out humbly!

Check out these Scriptures about how to control your thoughts:

- ✓ 2 Corinthians 10:3-5
- ✓ 2 Corinthians 5:13
- ✓ Ephesians 5:18-20
- ✓ Proverbs 23:7
- ✓ Luke 10:17-21
- ✓ 1 Thessalonians 5:18
- ✓ Philippians 3:13-14

- ✓ Philippians 4:7,8, 13
- ✓ Hebrews 12:1-2
- ✓ Romans 12:1-2

Humble communication begins with having a healthy thought life. That means making sacrifices and putting in the efforts of holding yourself accountable to Scripture, regularly taking an inventory of your own thoughts, and readily and easily changing those thoughts when corrected by the Holy Spirit. Below are 10 step-by-step instructions on how to control your thoughts:

1.) Write down your thoughts to take them captive. This allows you to see your thoughts for what they are and not hide any of them in the darkness.
2.) Recognize their root: Holy Spirit, or enemy? Take those written down thoughts and examine their motives. Are they fear or faith based?
3.) Erase it or mark through it. For those thoughts you have written down that do not line up with Scripture, literally mark through them.
4.) What would the Lord say or not say? Understand why the thoughts you marked through do not line up with Scripture.

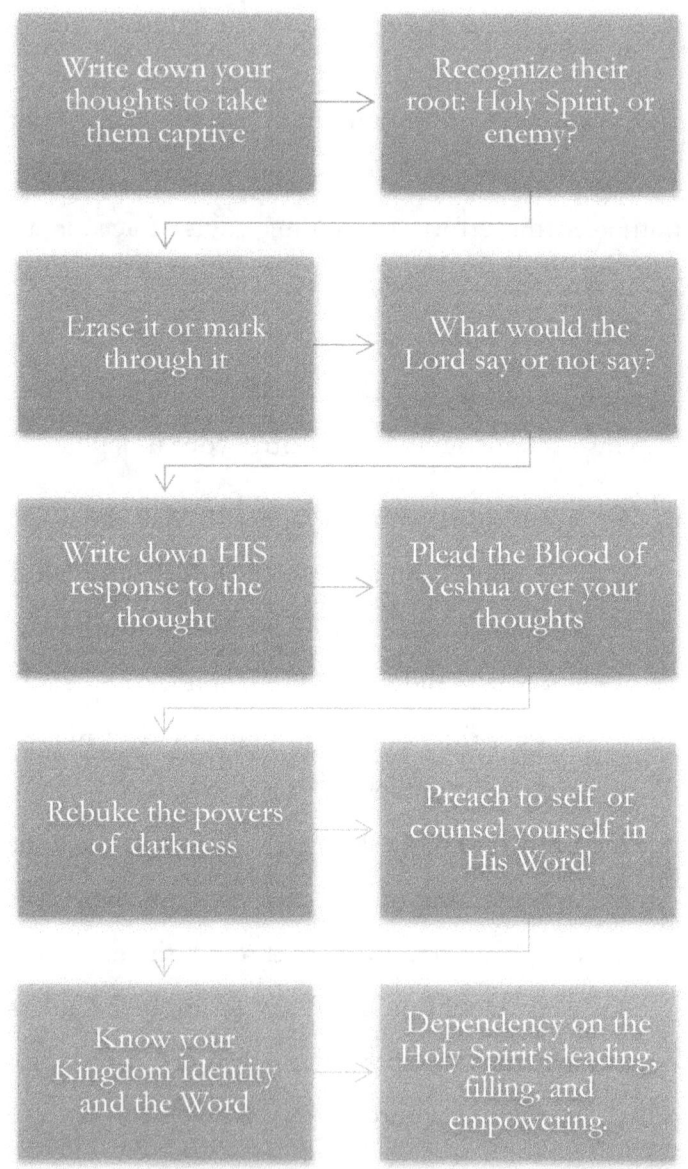

5.) Write down HIS response to the thought. Replace the marked out thought with HIS thoughts by writing down the corroborated Scripture.

6.) Plead the Blood of Yeshua over your thoughts. This is literal. Ask God fervently to cover your thoughts in the Blood of His Son.

7.) Rebuke the powers of darkness. Remove the powers and influence they have in your thoughts by repenting and rebuking!

8.) Preach to self or counsel yourself in His Word. Preach to yourself if your emotions are having a difficult time letting go of the wrong thoughts.

9.) Know your Kingdom Identity and the Word. Spend lots of time studying your Kingdom Identity so you have a firm grasp on who you are; when you know who you are, your thoughts are in line with that identity!

10.) Dependency on the Holy Spirit's leading, filling, and empowering. The last and final step of controlling your thoughts is becoming dependent upon the Holy Spirit to lead, fill, and empower you in times when your flesh is weak. Take a moment of silence to listen for His Voice to guide you through a tough conversation!

Review:

Do you understand that your thoughts are influenced by the things you hear and see?

_____
_____
_____

What is one of the biggest negative thoughts you struggle with today?

_____
_____
_____

What Scriptures can you find to encourage you about that negative thought and replace it with?

_____
_____
_____

Have you ever been guilty of thinking ill of someone, and then found out that you later couldn't communicate with them properly because of your negative thoughts about them? If so, how can you remedy that situation for the future?

_____

_____
_____

Chapter Twelve

Diversified Definition:

Body Language. The process of communicating nonverbally through conscious or unconscious gestures and movements.

Body language is as important as verbal language. You can be saying something nice, but if your body language is intimidating or hostile, the person you are communicating with won't even hear what you are saying. Body language often can be an even stronger indicator of the intentions and purpose of the person communicating than the verbal words that are spoken, or the tone of voice.

> The fact of the matter is, the more capable we are, the humbler we should be.
>
> Jeffrey R. Holland

Body language is more involuntary than speech or tone. While you may be able to hide something by masking your tone of voice or choosing different words to speak, your body language is harder to hide and takes more focus and discipline to consciously mask. Body language will always be a result of what you are thinking about and what emotion that thought provokes.

In humble communication, paying attention to your own body language as well as the other person is extremely important. Knowing how to discern and read body language of others can help you understand things about what they are feeling or thinking that they may be too afraid or uncomfortable to talk about verbally.

Body language can show when a person is lying, if you know how to read the indicators properly. This can be useful in business communications, as well as personal relationships. Humble communication involves speaking the truth and discerning the lie. These body language indicators should be taken note of carefully; remember that the most powerful tool and gift you have in reading body language is the discernment of the Holy Spirit.

Common Body Language Indicators:

- ✓ Raised eyebrows often signal discomfort

- Shaky legs indicate nervousness
- Crossed legs can be a sign of low receptivity and resistance
- Involved laughter (laughing with you not at you) is a sign of genuine interest
- Eye contact can show both positive and negative interest, depending on the depth, length, and overall vibe of the contact
- If their voice goes up or down, it is a sign of interest
- Lack of wrinkles or crinkles around the corners of the mouth while smiling indicate a fake smile
- If the other person is mirroring your body language, that is an indicator of the conversation going well
- Expansive, authoritive postures with shoulders back and neck straight (without a hunch) indicate leadership and confidence
- Direct eye contact for too long indicates lying
- Slouching can be an indicator of boredom or laziness
- Narrowing of the lips and furrowing of the eyebrows indicates anger
- Lips stretched slightly back towards the ears, as well as raised upper eyelids indicate fear
- Drooping upper eyelids and a slight pulling downwards of the corners of the lips indicate sadness

- ✓ Upper lip raised and nose wrinkling indicates disgust
- ✓ Genuine happiness has indicators of raised cheeks, crow's feet wrinkles around eyes, and movement from muscle that orbits the eye
- ✓ An open mouth with widened eyes indicates surprise
- ✓ A lip corner that is tightened and raised on only one side indicates contempt
- ✓ If the feet of the person you're talking to are pointed away from you, chances are they are ready to bolt from the conversation
- ✓ Arms that are propped on hips and spread out indicate authority and "issues" that need to be discussed
- ✓ Arms behind the back generally indicates trying to keep others at bay
- ✓ Someone whose body language allows closeness or sitting close to you is more than likely more comfortable with you than someone who keeps their distance physically when speaking
- ✓ Leaning forward and having open arms or open body language indicates responsiveness
- ✓ Clenched fists and pointed fingers as well as leaning forward can show signs of aggression

- ✓ Chin stroking can indicate thoughtfulness and consideration
- ✓ Body language that indicates listening includes a tilted head, nodding, frequent eye contact, and high blinking rate
- ✓ Combative body language includes finger tapping, staring, and foot tapping

There are many more indicators than this, however, the more time you spend discerning what kinds of postures and body language send out what kinds of signals, the more apt you are to pick up on other, even more hidden body signals. If you can tell something you are saying is making someone uncomfortable by their body language, you can salvage the conversation by switching subjects or changing tone of voice.

Body language is important for many reasons, but the biggest reason is that it is beneficial to have genuine, truth-filled, humble communications in both business and personal relationships. Body language will either reveal things the other person is trying to hide, or affirm things they are already saying are true.

In a business situation, if you could tell that someone was lying to you by their body language, it would be a great indicator to the quality of the business they will bring you.

However, it's also important not to project your perception onto others merely based on body language. If you're having trouble discerning, it's better to ask questions than assume.

Part of humble communication is the willingness to ask and answer questions that are asked. Prideful people don't like to answer or be asked questions; if questions seem to irritate the person you are having a conversation with, that can be an indicator that they are hiding something or are having anger issues elsewhere in life.

Review:

Do you make it a habit to interpret and pay attention to other people's body language when having a conversation?

_____
_____
_____

What is one of the most confusing body language indicators to you and why?

_____
_____
_____

What body language of others do you have the easiest time reading and why?

_____

_____

_____

Do you think others have an easy time reading your body language? Why or why not?

_____

_____

_____

Chapter Thirteen

Diversified Definition:

Listening. To give one's attention to a sound; more importantly, to hear what someone is saying and offer a relevant response.

Listening is also perhaps one of the most important aspects to humble communication. Others that you have conversations with will want to know and feel as if you are genuinely listening to them and their concerns. If the other person does not feel listened to, it may cause strife in the relationship.

This is something you also want to receive when you are communicating with someone else: them genuinely listening to what you have to say. Below are some active listening skills you can practice to enhance your humble communication:

- ✓ Use minimal encouragers.
- ✓ Ask open-ended questions

- ✓ Paraphrase
- ✓ Pause Effectively
- ✓ Reflect/mirror
- ✓ Label emotions
- ✓ Use "I" messages
- ✓ Summarize

Using minimal encouragers through the conversation such as "uh-huh", "yeah", or "okay" indicate that you are present and listening actively. When someone is articulating a prolonged thought, minimal encouragers let the speaker know that you are paying attention and not losing focus or interest.

> The humble man makes room for progress; the proud man believes he is already there.
>
> Ed Parker

Asking open-ended questions allows the speaker to give further details and gives the impression that the listener is genuinely interested in the topic of conversation. It conveys the idea that the listener is trying to gain understanding of the speaker.

Paraphrasing is simply restating what the speaker said in your own words to affirm that you were listening and that you understand their purpose in communicating to you.

Awkward silences can be avoided in listening and conversations if the listener pauses effectively. This means giving the speaker a few seconds after they are done speaking to make sure they are finished, as well as giving the indication that you are allowing their words to sink in for better understanding.

Repeating the last few words a person said helps the speaker to continue their train of thought without being distracted or thinking that you have gotten distracted. Reflecting/mirroring a few of their words affirms that you are hearing what they are saying and are interested.

Labeling emotions is important for a listener if you are not able to discern the tone of the speaker's voice. If you're unsure, say things like, "You sound frustrated", or "I think you're upset". This gives the speaker the opportunity to clarify and helps you better understand their true intent instead of assuming.

Instead of saying "you" in conversations, use "I" to ease the atmosphere and make the speaker understand you are not accusing them. Say things like "I feel", instead of "you" to eliminate accusatory tones and indicators.

Periodically stopping the person who is speaking and summarizing what you have heard so far helps you to stay on track with what they are saying, and indicates to the speaker that you are genuinely interested in what they are saying. Be careful not to jump to problem solving or jump topics so the speaker doesn't feel like you are rushing them.

Another important factor for listening is to make sure that you're not applying judgment hastily, and that you're listening fully and not only to half-information. Selective hearing is a killer to humble communication. Selective hearing is when you have tuned your brain to only hear certain tones of voices or words. Your brain literally blocks out other important information to zero in on those preconceived notions you listen for.

Review:

Do other people consider you a good listener? Why or why not?

_____
_____
_____

How do you think you can make your humble communication better by listening better?

_____

_____

_____

Do you have a problem with selective hearing?

_____

_____

_____

Chapter Fourteen

Diversified Definition:

Distraction. Extreme agitation of the mind and emotions. A thing that prevents someone from giving their full attention to something else.

The enemy uses many distractions to try and thwart any plan we have for humbly communicating to another person. The enemy's favorite pastime is creating strife between people and using their own weaknesses against them to do it. There are many distractions the enemy offers to people to prevent them from communicating in an effective, humble manner:

- → Pride
- → Itching Ears
- → Envy
- → Lusting
- → Division
- → Disappointment

→ Discouragement

Pride is an extremely dangerous distraction from humble communication in the fact that pride not only shuts us off from being close to God and hearing from the Holy Spirit, but it also prevents us from hearing things that don't fit within our prideful perimeters. Pride is any manner of puffing oneself up above another, and lifting our own knowledge above the knowledge of God. When we are being prideful in our speech and actions, we are being distracted from humbly communicating.

Itching ears are ears that only hear what they want to hear. They are quick to listen to gossip and quick to shut off others that do not agree with their perspective. Itching ears only want to hear things that are smooth and unbothersome to the listener, and can be very effective in working against humble communication, which requires open ears.

Envy is another great blocker to humble communication. Envy creates a selfish sense of fairness and is offended when that fairness is not attributed to them. Envy causes people to murder others to obtain the object of their envy and can be a very effective distraction away from humble communication. When one envies another, they have the tendency to manipulate conversations for preferred outcomes.

Lusting is a lot like envy, but deals with sexual desires

> Kindness in words creates confidence. Kindness in thinking creates profoundness. Kindness in giving creates love.
>
> Lao Tzu

and other forbidden pleasures. When someone uses lustful communication, it can be very distracting from humble communication and leads the other person astray.

Division is a distraction that causes humble communication to crumble. Division is caused by doubt and worry and can cause us to abandon our loyalties and moral stances.

Disappointment comes when our expectations are not fulfilled and can be another effective distraction against humble communication. When we are disappointed, we tend to lead the conversations emotionally instead of rationally, as well as focus inwardly instead of on others.

Discouragement removes hope. It is devastating to humble communication because it doesn't allow room for improvement or comfort.

How to resist distractions:

- → Be Sober
- → Be Vigilant
- → Be Steadfast in Faith
- → Firmly Resist
- → Focus on Purpose

Being sober means being mentally alert and self-controlled, able to make sound decisions. Being vigilant means be watchful, awake, and alert. Putting these two together, we can learn how to resist distractions by making sure we are mentally alert and controlling our emotions, being watchful of possible doorways of distractions and avoiding them.

Being steadfast in faith means taking firm-footed actions to resist distractions. Removing yourself from bad company, alluring atmospheres, and distracting emotional situations. Anything that pulls us away from our moral center should be eliminated.

Firmly resisting distractions means standing up to anyone or anything that causes the distraction, and not panicking or taking flight at the first sign of the enemy's strategies. Communicate or take actions that would remedy the distraction.

Focusing on your purpose in communicating will also help you resist distractions and shut out unnecessary, hindering things. Lions make sure to rest and relax all day long so they are ready for the hunt at night. We should do the same thing when looking to humbly communicate and resist distractions.

Review:

Are you easily distracted when communicating or listening to others? If so, what are the things that most easily distract you and why?

_____
_____
_____

How can you remember your purpose in communicating better to avoid distractions?

_____
_____
_____

Do you have itching ears? If so, how can you remedy the problem?

_____

Chapter Fifteen

Diversified Definition:

Rebuke. An expression of sharp disapproval or criticism.

It is important to remember that people are not the enemy. Although people often are the sources of our pain, anger, and hurt because of their wrong actions or words, it is important to remember one vital thing: we are not at war with flesh and blood, but with the principalities and principles of the air (Ephesians 6:12).

When humbly communicating, it is important to remember that people are not our enemy. Although people can be used by the enemy to harm us, hurt us, cause us emotional or physical pain, the persons themselves are still human beings that God desires to see redeemed. If we allow ourselves the fleshly luxury of treating anyone ill based off our emotions or how the other person treated us, we would never be able to achieve humble communication, or be pleasing to God!

Sometimes even other believers who live their lives founded on the Word of God can be used by the enemy to hurt others. How does that happen? When that person is walking in rebellion or unrepentiveness, not confessing and repenting from their sin. It can also happen through ignorance and a lack of discernment, or simply because that person is acting in the flesh and not being controlled by the mind of the Holy Spirit.

> Without communication, there is no relationship.
>
> Author Unknown

It's important to remember that if someone hurt you, the best thing you can do is continue to humbly communicate, bless, and not hold it against that person. Choose to remain firmly footed in your humility, and ask God to bless them with understanding and repentance.

To ensure that you are not the source of causing others pain by not humbly communicating, you should practice rebuking the real enemy daily.

In the Name of Yeshua (Jesus) and by the power of the Holy Spirit, I rebuke:

- ✓ Satan
- ✓ Grudges
- ✓ Demonic forces
- ✓ Evil influences
- ✓ Depression
- ✓ Anxiety
- ✓ Fears
- ✓ Pride
- ✓ Lies
- ✓ Deception
- ✓ Control
- ✓ Manipulation
- ✓ My words
- ✓ My flesh
- ✓ My opinions
- ✓ False perceptions
- ✓ False judgments
- ✓ Hidden intentions
- ✓ Impure motivations

Rebuking these things, and anything else in your life that does not line up with the Word of God in the Name of Yeshua (Jesus) exercises the power you have been given over the powers of darkness through the Holy Spirit and your applied faith.

Rebuking these things ahead of time will help you be prepared to guard against distractions as such that will work against your humble communication and cause strife in your relationships. Even if you are not in the habit of rebuking things out loud like this, now is a good time to start so you are able to discover and apply in the future the power of rebuking the enemy!

Review:

Are there any things on the rebuke list that currently plague your life? If so, which ones?

_____
_____
_____

Do you have an issue with always looking at people as the problem instead of the real enemy behind the scenes? If so, how can you remedy that?

_____
_____
_____

Have you ever practiced the principle of rebuking before, and if not, what have you noticed afterwards?

_____

_____

_____

Chapter Sixteen

Diversified Definition:

Attitude. A settled way of thinking or feeling about someone or something, typically one that is reflected in a person's behavior. A position of the body proper to or implying an action or mental state.

Humble communication requires a humble attitude.

> *Communication must be HOT. Honest, Open, and Two-Way. – Dan Oswald*

Attitude determines everything about how a person communicates; what their body language looks like, what their tone sounds like, and the meaning of the words they choose. Attitude is pertinent to every action we take in life, because attitude can tell us more about the motivation and heart intention behind why we do what we do.

Attitudes determine our failure or success. Attitude determines the kind of company we keep. Attitude determines how others perceive us upon a first impression. Wrong attitudes lead to abusive behaviors as well as painful consequences in our relationships. Right attitudes lead to positive, uplifting behaviors as well as encouraging, prosperous, and fruitful consequences in our relationships.

There are many things to consider about your attitude as you learn humble communication. You should make a regular habit of putting your attitude into check and making sure it fits the criteria of a humble attitude:

→ Low opinion of oneself; motivation to communicate is not for self-elevation
→ High opinion of others; motivation to communicate is for uplifting and edifying others
→ Heavenly focused; motivation to communicate is for glorifying God and spreading the Good News of His Son
→ Empathetic; motivation to communicate is for comforting others or helping others solve problems
→ Wholesome; motivations to communicate are not birthed from hidden agendas or secret intentions of manipulating the will of others
→ Truthful; motivation to communicate is for sharing truthful facts and information that is pertinent to the lives of others

Humble communication is about having the right heart attitude behind why you're saying what you're saying. People have found ways to mask their words, their facial expressions, their tones of voices, as well as their body language, to hide the intent of their heart, but people cannot change the energy they create by their inward heart attitude.

Attitudes are a powerful force, and we should learn how to control them in communication. Let's review a few things about attitudes that you may not have known:

- ✓ A right attitude can change the circumstances around you for the better
- ✓ A right attitude can be the key to victory in hard and pressing circumstances
- ✓ A wrong attitude affects even the way you walk, as well as every other posture in your body
- ✓ No one else can change your attitude for you; only you can do that
- ✓ The Holy Spirit is the One who empowers us to have the ability to have a right attitude
- ✓ Your attitude is determined by the things you focus on in your thoughts
- ✓ Prayer always increases and anoints our attitude to be right with God

- ✓ Your experiences with God are based on your attitude towards Him
- ✓ Focusing on the goodness of God corrects our wrong attitudes
- ✓ Wrong attitudes can be rectified by changing the focus of your thoughts
- ✓ The atmosphere of your life and the experiences you have are determined by your attitude
- ✓ Persistent attitudes can cause major changes in situations that have become idle
- ✓ Every relationship in your life is affected by your right or wrong attitudes
- ✓ Miracles are either welcomed or hindered based on right or wrong attitudes
- ✓ People are attracted into your life based on your attitude; right attitudes attract the right people, wrong attitudes attract the wrong people
- ✓ Wrong attitudes can sometimes be created from false memories
- ✓ If you want to change your attitude, you must first change what you know

If you're having problems in your relationships because of communication issues, then it's time to start examining the attitudes in your life that are creating this outcome. If you have a wrong attitude towards someone, it could be the source of a wrong thought, a false memory, or a "preconceived notion", which is a thought that is formed before all the information has been presented.

Chances are, if you have a wrong attitude towards a person it is affecting your ability to humbly communicate with them. If this is the case, it is vital that you take the steps needed to change wrong attitudes. Look:

- ☐ Meditate on God's Word; study Scriptures that relate specifically to the attitude you are having (pride, jealousy, anger, etc.).
- ☐ Listen to uplifting music and take the time to praise God and thank Him. Worship.
- ☐ Pursue only assignments that the Holy Spirit has given you instead of making your own plans and goals.
- ☐ Make consistent time to meet with God daily, and refuse to miss it for anything in the world.

Attitudes can make all the difference in your relationships and your ability to communicate properly in them. If you notice yourself having wrong attitudes, don't ignore it and hope it will go away; be proactive about remedying the attitude and ask forgiveness from anyone who may have been affected.

Review:

Are there any wrong attitudes in my life? If so, what are they, and which relationships are affected?

___

What is one daily practice I am willing to commit to put my attitude into check?

___

Is it difficult for me to change my attitude? Why or why not?

___

Chapter Seventeen

Diversified Definition:

Emotion. An emotion is a natural instinctive state of mind deriving from one's circumstances, mood, or relationships with others.

Emotions also affect our communication skills. Emotions that are not rooted in humility and love will destroy conversations and relationships through wrong behaviors and actions. Emotions are direct contributors to our attitudes.

> *The art of communication is the language of leadership. – James Humes*

It is vital to understand how to recognize, control, and change emotions when needed. Humble communication hinges on the ability to change emotions when difficult situations arise, and being able to think clearly and make sound decisions in the middle of chaos without being emotional in the moment.

Emotions are given to us for a reason, and can be the direct result of what we have been thinking about. Emotions are like warning signs or confirmation signs that are telling us everything is in balance, or something is off balance. Once we learn how to discern the root of an emotion, we can either validate it, or eliminate it.

Emotions that should be eliminated but are instead acted upon and focused on create wrong attitudes, affect our communication skills, and wreak havoc in our relationships. We can literally cause others to suffer due to acting on wrong emotions that are invalidated but acted upon as if validated.

Six Steps to Mastering Emotions:

→ Root It Out. Identify the root of the emotion. Where did it come from, and what purpose does it serve? What thought created this emotion? Was that thought founded in love, or selfishness?
→ Follow the Root. Discern how this emotion will affect others if acted upon. How will this emotion enhance or depress my life and the life of others?
→ Interrogate It. Don't give the emotion any room to breathe. Interrogate it until you have asked every

relevant question necessary to determine the root motivation of this emotion. Do I desire to feel this way? What thoughts am I willing to change to change how I feel?

→ Be the Boss of It. Those emotions don't control you! You control them. You're in charge of those emotions and what they're allowed to accomplish and not allowed to accomplish.

→ Plan to Meet It Again. More than likely, this emotion will pop up again given the opportunity, or if those thoughts that sparked the emotion are thought upon again. Mentally prepare yourself to encounter this emotion again and know how to change it if needed.

→ Kick It into Gear! Be optimistic about change and allow yourself to get excited about being in control of your emotions. Discipline your thoughts to discipline and control your emotions!

How to Recognize the Purpose of An Emotion:

If You Feel…

Lonely → You need more interaction with people.

Angry → An important moral rule of yours has been broken; communicate your moral needs with others.

Uncomfortable → You need to change your thinking habits, clarify your purpose, and take different action.

Inadequate → You need to reexamine your standards and adjust them, or you may need to put more effort into things.

Fearful → You need to prepare yourself for action.

Overwhelmed or Depressed → You need to prioritize what is important in your life.

Hurt → Your expectations are not being met and you need to communicate them.

Disappointed → Your expectations may need to change.

Guilty or Regretful → You may have violated one of your own standards.

Empowering Emotions:

- ☐ Emotion of Contribution (you desire to add value and contribute to solutions)
- ☐ Love and Warmth
- ☐ Emotion of Vitality (you have energy and endurance)
- ☐ Gratitude and Appreciation
- ☐ Cheerfulness (the ability to be joyful when in tough situations)

- ☐ Emotion of Curiosity (you are curious enough to research the truth)
- ☐ Confidence
- ☐ Passion and Zeal (excitement)
- ☐ Flexibility (the ability to easily adjust your expectations/desires)
- ☐ Determination (the attitude of never giving up)

Review:

Which emotions do I have the hardest time changing and why?

_____
_____
_____

What thoughts affect my emotions for the worst the most?

_____
_____
_____

What thoughts affect my emotions for the better the most?

_____
_____
_____

Chapter Eighteen

Diversified Definition:

Humility. Humility is a modest or low view of one's own importance; humbleness.

The Bible says that God resists the proud and gives grace to the humble (1 Peter 5:5-6). Humility is necessary to be close to God, to walk in love, to learn, to grow, to add value to the lives of others, to receive gifts from the Holy Spirit, and to have healthy relationships that are peace-filled and not strife-filled.

Humility involves lowering your opinion of yourself, putting yourself on a lower priority than others, preferring others over yourself, and doing things to purposely elevate others. Humility involves considering the needs of others before you consider your own needs, and purposely sacrificing things that you can to meet a need of someone else's.

Humility recognizes its need to learn, be corrected, and to be given grace. Pride blocks understanding, enhances negative emotions, and fills communication with confusion and pain. The results of a pride-filled conversation would more than likely be a fist fight between two people, or at the very least a heated argument, whereas a humble conversation would show conflict resolution, empathy, and peace.

Let's look at an acrostic for the word "communication":

C – Consideration of others

O – Observation of others

M – Muting harmful emotions

M – Meditating positive thoughts

U – Understanding others' perspectives

N – Negotiating solutions

I – Inquiring for information

C – Careful choice of words

A – Attention to detail

T – Truth only

I – Investigating issues

O – Ongoing willingness to change

N – Nurturing niceness

Consideration of others is a vital first step that will help you walk in humility if you are having a hard time coming out of being prideful. Considering others means thinking about what it must be like to walk a mile in their shoes; considering their emotions, viewpoints, and opinions instead of disregarding them.

Observing others will help you understand more about their character. Their posture, speech, habits, and the way they treat others will give you insight into the things they are strong and weak in. Observing others will also help you discern the atmosphere of the conversation and steer it in the right direction.

Muting harmful emotions means not acting on them, and putting them to the back of your mind until you can invest the time into finding their source. Muting harmful emotions in the middle of a heated conversation can be a little tricky, but will also lead the way to victory and conflict resolution.

Meditating on positive thoughts will allow your mind to stay focused on the things the Bible instructs us to focus on; pure, lovely, wholesome, true, noble, right thoughts (Philippians 4:8). This will in turn affect your emotions and your behaviors during conversations, which will allow the conversation to remain humble and peaceful.

Understanding other's perspectives is important in humble communication because conversations are not one-sided, they are two-sided. Humble communication always includes the perspectives of others and never discounts or demands that one side is seen over the other.

> *Communication leads to community, that is, to understanding, intimacy, and mutual valuing. – Rollo May*

Negotiating solutions means going over possible remedies for the issue that are favorable for everyone, not just one party over another. Negotiating solutions means having two willing parties and not just one that is willing to compromise their stance for the sake of a resolution.

Inquiring for information allows the speaker to give more details, and helps the listener to understand the subject of conversation more in depth. It can also lengthen the conversation, so both parties feel more successful afterwards.

Careful choice of words is an obvious ingredient to humble communication, as each word has specific meaning, and choosing the wrong word may lead to pain, confusion, and strife. Choosing proper words and paying special attention to tone can ensure that every conversation you have turns out for the best!

Attention to detail is vital in humble communication, as even the smallest details can sometimes make the biggest difference. Remembering details from specific conversations can also help later throughout your relationship with the person you had the conversation with.

Speaking truth only will ensure that your humble communication is proper and delivered for the right reasons. Lies can be difficult to keep up with and make relationships and communication confusing. Speaking only truth is the best way to communication personally and in a business setting.

Investigating issues could entail asking more detailed questions, remembering details of previous conversations, and recalling reasons for any negative emotions that have come because of that issue. Investigating issues in humble communication will ensure that the strife is removed as quickly as possible.

Having an ongoing willingness to change is also vital in humble communication, because sometimes our point of view needs to be changed to come to a workable resolution. Not being willing to change is a sign of pride and automatically cancels out any hope of a humble conversation.

Nurturing niceness is a great way to keep the negative emotions at bay, keep your tone positive, your posture straight, and sealing the conversation with a good ending. Nurturing niceness would include only allowing yourself to think and say positive things for the edification of the listener. It also includes being more creative with how you deliver critical comments, or communication that involves correcting the other person.

Humility, as you can see, is vital in communicating all the way around because humility is an open door that allows positivity and hope to reign supreme in a conversation instead of doom and gloom. Having communication that revolves around solving problems rather than rehashing them is also more beneficial to relationships.

Review:

Which letter on the communication acrostic do I have the hardest time with and why?

_____
_____
_____

Which letter on the communication acrostic do I have the easiest time with and why?

_____

On a scale from 1 to 10, 1 being the lowest and 10 being the highest, how humble are my daily conversations, and what can I do to make them humbler on a regular basis?

Chapter Nineteen

Diversified Definition:

Conversation. The informal exchange of ideas by spoken words.

Conversations hold many purposes. The main purpose is to communicate ideas to one another. Conversations can also take the form of problem solving, inspiration for the future, comforting one another, encouraging one another, correcting one another, teaching one another, and healing one another.

Conversations should never be used to impose negativities in the lives of others. Conversations should always be pointed towards resolutions and uplifting, edifying matters. It's alright to have conversations

> *Only through communication can human life hold meaning. – Paulo Freire*

about pain, hurt, trauma, and the like, if those conversations lead to healing and resolution for the people having them.

Conversations should be a way to release, restore, reconfigure, and recognize; release ideas, restore pains, reconfigure problems, and recognize solutions. The misuse of conversations leads to many of the world's problems today; people aspiring to do crime and wickedness together, gossiping, spreading lies, and any other manner of negative, abusive reasonings.

Here are a few tips to remember in your conversations:

→ Never speak while someone else is speaking. It's not only rude; neither party can hear what the other is saying if more than one person is talking at a time.
→ Don't allow your thoughts to wander. Keep a straight focus while you are listening to the other person speaking, so when it's your turn to speak, you're in line with the topic of conversation. Wandering thoughts lead to broken conversations.
→ Avoid assumptions. Assumptions lead to expectations of understanding; you should never assume that someone else understands what you have said.
→ Don't take part in conversations that lead to trivial things. Small talk is alright if you're among strangers,

but when doing business or in a professional setting, too much small talk is not polite or appropriate.

→ If someone is mumbling, encourage them to speak up. Don't pretend like you're heard something that someone has said if you didn't. It's better to ask them to speak up and repeat themselves.

→ Be careful to speak at the appropriate volume for the noise in the room. You want to avoid others having to ask you to repeat yourself by speaking clearly and concisely.

→ Discern who you have conversations with about the deep inner workings of your life. Don't speak your opinion unless asked for it, and be careful not to unequally yoke yourself in conversation with someone who doesn't care about what you have to say.

→ Every word matters. If you're having trouble finding the right one, it's perfectly acceptable to stop in the middle of the conversation to search out the right word before moving on. Communicate your desire to find the right word so the listener understands.

The words we choose when having conversations are vital. Words can hurt, heal, confuse, clarify, create problems, or solve them. A person of wisdom considers their words before speaking them. They count the cost of what those words will accomplish, and what must be paid to speak and hear them.

A person of wisdom understands that words affect the accumulation or lack of wealth. The power of life and death are in the tongue (Proverbs 18:21), and whatever words you choose to speak are the words that you will eat the fruit of.

A person of wisdom understands that the right words can uplift those around them, and the wrong words can depress those around them. Words can be freeing or implements of prison and bondage. The right words can also get you through any situation or any position of trouble.

A person of wisdom does not praise themselves, but allows others to uplift them. Wisdom doesn't allow its host to boast or puff itself up, so a person of wisdom will never walk around talking about their own excellence.

A person of wisdom also understands that receiving or rejecting words spoken into their lives can either create blessings or create chaos. Words spoken into your life should be in line with the Bible, and not negativity or demonic influences.

Overall, humble communication will consist of humble conversations; guard your conversations by guarding your words! Choose wisely and carefully, and don't rush into conversations you're not prepared to have with excellence. Invest time into preparing yourself for every conversation, and you'll always find the result to be humble, positive, and solution oriented!

Review:

What do most of your conversations consist of?

_____
_____
_____

On a scale from 1 to 10, 1 being the lowest and 10 being the highest, how carefully do you choose your words before speaking them?

_____
_____
_____

How many of your conversations end with chaos, and how many with peace? What do you think the major failing point of your conversations are, and what can you do to fix it?

_____
_____
_____

Chapter Twenty

Diversified Definition:

Mediation. Intervention in a dispute in order to resolve it; arbitration.

Mediation can take place without any legal measures; arbitration is a step up from mediation in that it involves legal professionals to settle disputes. Mediation can be as simple as calling in a neutral friend to hear out a matter between friends; the mediator would hold no biased opinions, but hold each party accountable for their attitudes and tones, and maintain a peaceful communication between the two parties.

> It's not distance that keeps people apart; it's lack of communication. – Author Unknown

If you find yourself in the position of being a mediator between two people, here are some important facts to consider:

- → The need for a mediator means that the two parties were unsuccessful in the negotiation process. Therefore, mediation is not a cooperative situation as negotiation is, but can be quite competitive.
- → Don't create an "anchor" by speaking a possible solution before the mediation has even begun. This creates a possible stopping point for the mediation process and can make things become quite stagnant.
- → Avoid debating things over a telephone. Be careful how you speak about each party and do not reveal weaknesses or present things as weaknesses. If there is more than one mediator involved in the situation, all mediators should be careful how they speak amongst themselves about the situation.
- → Do not become overconfident. The mediation process is about settling disputes, not creating a pedestal for the mediator. Focus on the task at hand and not your awesome mediation skills.
- → Evaluate the situation completely before beginning the mediation process. You need to have a clear and concise understanding of the situation before entering into the mediation process.
- → Draft a good mediation summary. Be prepared with the words you will choose when mediating.

- → Set bargaining points and know ahead of time what issues will be more lenient and which will be more stringent.
- → Keep your emotions in balance and be emotionally detached from both the situation and the outcome. Emotions can plague sound judgment.
- → Take your time to settle the agreements. Mediation can be a lengthy and arduous process. It can also go smoothly and end shortly, depending on the situation and the experience of the mediators, as well as the attitudes of the parties entering mediation.

Mediation can be a scary task to perform if you're not prepared ahead of time with how to work towards an accomplished resolution. Mediation can also be a scary task to perform if you're not understanding of the situation, or facts are confusing and muddled. In mediation situations like that, you should take your time to sort things out and refuse to settle for anything less than your best.

Review:

Have you ever needed mediation in a situation? If so, why?

_____
_____
_____

Have you ever mediated for someone else in a situation? Why or why not?

_____
_____
_____

Is there a situation in your life right now that you feel would be best resolved by mediation? If so, why?

_____
_____
_____

Chapter Twenty-One

Communication Goals

Below, write out 3 goals for yourself on how you would like to achieve humble communication in your relationships:

My Top 3 Communication Goals for Humbler Communication:

The ABCs to Communication During Confrontation:

A – Attitude is everything

B – Believe

C – Compassionate towards others

D – Documentation

E – Expectations are clear

F – Forgive either way

G – Guard your heart and mind

H – Humility brings favor

I – Information

J – Jesus to them, see Jesus in them

K – Kingdom Principles

L – Legacy focused

M – Motivational illustrations and testimonies

N – Negotiation

O – Order reveals honor and integrity

P – Preparation

Q – Quality questions

R – Reward focused

S – Solution focused

T – Timing and time management

U – Unified

V – Value their heart, need, time, and ideas

W – Will of God

X – X-ray true motives

Y – Yield to the Holy Spirit

Z – Zealous

When humbly communicating, remember that Attitude is Everything! The right attitude can lead to solutions, and the wrong attitude can sting!

Believe what the other person is saying is true, and put weight and consideration into what they say and do. Believe they are trying their best to communicate humbly with you, and believe that you can too!

Be Compassionate Towards Others when humbly communicating, and others will be blessed by the love you are creating! Even in times of confrontation, compassion is as important as the words you choose; in the end, if you're not loving, you have everything to lose!

Have Documentation to back up the things you are saying; present facts without negative emotion or attitude, and the other person will hear what you are relaying.

Make sure your Expectations are Always Clear when in a confrontation, as knowing what the other person's expectations are helps for better relation.

Forgive Either Way, no matter how the confrontation turns out. Never leave room on your part for the consequences of unforgiveness and doubt!

Guard your heart and mind against the enemy and his devices; keep yourself centered in Yeshua (Jesus), and purposely make self-sacrifices. In humble communication, the enemy will try to work against your humility with control, manipulation, intimidation, domination, and seduction. Guard your heart and mind in God's Word, and He'll save your conversations from destruction!

Remember that Humility Brings Favor in confrontations and in life. Humility is the element that ushers in peace and removes strife!

Make sure your Information is accurate and presented with clarity and care; never alter information to give yourself favor, but let integrity be your pair!

Be Jesus to Them and See Jesus in Them during times of confrontation; this will help you remain spiritually focused and have humble communication!

Use Kingdom Principles to remain humble in confrontations, such as treating others the way you would want to be treated. This will help you remain calm when things get a little heated!

Be Legacy Focused when in a confrontation of any kind; ask yourself if the legacy of your behavior is something you will be proud to leave behind.

Use Motivational Illustrations and Testimonies when in confrontations that are relevant to the subject; using examples of real life situations is something most people won't reject!

Remember the principles of Negotiation when the confrontation comes; remain humble for the ultimate, favored outcome!

Remember that order reveals honor and integrity; this is how God designed you and me to be! When our hearts are in order, our words will follow through; if you have order, you'll already have honor and integrity too!

Preparation always helps when communicating; knowing your subject and the person you're talking to is better for relating. Prepare yourself mentally and emotionally to have successful, humble conversations; preparation always has an application!

Remember to ask quality questions in your conversations, which include open-ended questions that show your interest. In return, the other person you're talking to will be sure to give you their best!

When in a confrontation, remember to stay focused on the reward; this will keep you humble and help everyone be in one accord!

Remaining focused on solutions is always important when in confrontations, too. Otherwise, you may become so confused you won't be sure what to do!

Remember your timing and time management when in a confrontation; don't allow arguments and strife to continue, or the conversation will end in aggravation!

Unification is important in humble communication, especially when in a confrontation; being unified is the only way to have proper human relation!

Remember to value the other person's heart, time, need, and ideas when in a confrontation of any sorts; people are more concerned about how much you care than all the knowledge you exhort.

Make the will of God the center of all your confrontations; this will help you stay in humble communication!

Make sure to x-ray your true motives when communicating, so your heart doesn't lead you astray; make sure your words are founded in love and faith before you say what you have to say!

Always yield to the Holy Spirit when in a confrontation, no matter what. On the road to humble communications, there is no short cut!

Remain zealous in your passionate pursuit of humble communication; allow your dedication to be more important to you than your frustration!

Twelve Steps for Dealing with Conflict

By Tamara Lowe

1- Do your best to respond in love and not be provoked, so that the offending party may have nothing to legitimately accuse you of

2- Stand your ground. Having done all, stand (Eph. 6:13)

3- Be wise. do damage control. keep the sheep out of it all. preserve them.

4- Spiritual warfare: bind up the spirit of accusation (use this verse- it's so powerful: Isaiah 54:17)

5- The decent ones always repent. We forgive them and bless them now, and when they repent we receive and restore them.

6- BUT don't trust them again carte blanche. They have to earn that trust all over again because if they did it once, they can do it again.

7- It won't ever stop. the spiritual opposition is relentless. count it all joy. the devil is threatened so we must be doing something right.

8- God repeats His lessons as many times as we need them, so it's best to humbly seek the Lord for what we may be missing, what we've done wrong, and wholeheartedly repent if He shows us anything

9- Don't give up or give in. get zealous and fight hard.

10- Let forgiveness come easy to you. we don't fight against flesh and blood. the people are just tools and pawns. it's a spiritual battle, not an earthly one. So we have to use spiritual weapons and keep our hearts free of judgement, pride, sin, distraction, the love of money and the like.

11- Lean in to the Lord. Be on His side. Be about His business. Stay focused on His focus.

12- These types of conflicts are designed by hell to distract us. Don't buy into it. The more threats, accusations and intimidation are attached to the attack, the more truly irrelevant it is. Don't get worked up. That's what hell is hoping you'll do. Stay calm and stay the course.

For more Treasure Map titles by Dr. Chad Costantino, please visit:

www.abundantlifepublishing.org

www.ingramcontent.com/pod-product-compliance
Lightning Source LLC
Chambersburg PA
CBHW070250230526
45470CB00002B/553